Practical CLEMATIS GROWING

Ian Murray

The Crowood Pre

D0433002

First published in 1992 by
The Crowood Press Ltd
Ramsbury, Marlborough
Wiltshire SN8 2HR

© The Crowood Press Ltd 1992

British Library Cataloguing in Publication Data

A catalogue record for this book is available from the British
Library

ISBN 1 85223 656 6

Acknowledgements

Special thanks to Steve Bradley of Merristwood College of
Horticulture, Worplesdon, Surrey; Rex Cheatham, Mrs I.
Gibbon, Mrs B. Powell and Mrs A. MacWilliams of Bracknell
Horticultural Society; Mrs Anne Noble; Mrs Betty Risdon of
The International Clematis Society, Tropical Bird Gardens,
Rode, Nr. Bath, Somerset; Mrs L. Rutherford, Dorney Reach,
Buckinghamshire; Mrs Todhunter, Farnborough, Hampshire.
Thanks also to The Valley Clematis Nursery, Willingham
Road, Hainton, Lincolnshire, LN3 6LN for the photographs
on pages 9 (right), 13, 15, 16, 29 (left), 35 (top), 37 (left), 38,
43, 46 (left), 51, 53 and 55.
Other photographs by Sue Atkinson.
Line-drawings by Claire Upsdale-Jones.

Typeset by Chippendale Type Ltd, Otley, West Yorkshire
Printed and bound in Great Britain by
BPCC Hazell Books Ltd, Aylesbury

CONTENTS

INTRODUCTION   4

1 PLANTING   6
2 AFTERCARE AND CULTIVATION   11
3 SITE AND SUPPORT   14
4 CLEMATIS IN TUBS   26
5 PRUNING   29
6 PESTS AND OTHER PROBLEMS   39
7 FOR THE ENTHUSIAST   43
8 CHOOSING CLEMATIS   51

CLEMATIS CALENDAR   61
GLOSSARY   62
INDEX   64

INTRODUCTION

One of the greatest joys of a garden is the large diversity of plant life which can be successfully grown. Indeed, a wide range of subjects is essential to take advantage of the differing conditions which prevail. Large and small gardens have shady and sunny areas and the soil can vary from wet to dry and might comprise clay, sand, loam or any combination of these components. Some trees, shrubs and herbaceous plants have fairly specific requirements while others are happy in a variety of conditions, especially if they are carefully planted and maintained in a suitable manner.

Clematis fall into the adaptable category and they have the added versatility of enabling the embellishment of vertical surfaces. Every garden has walls and fences and many have other structures which would benefit from ornamental treatment. Of course, there are other climbing plants which fulfil this role, but I would suggest that none is superior to the clematis. Unlike some other subjects, which are loosely described as climbers, clematis have a true ability to cling to natural or man-made aids. Thus they are enabled to root in moist, shaded areas while the upper growth seeks the brightness of more elevated levels.

Not only do these plants provide flowers of considerable beauty, they also combine the virtues of hardiness, reliability and ease of cultivation; although there may be a widespread view to the contrary. Few people would deny that clematis blooms are enormously attractive and the large-flowered hybrids are universally appreciated, but there is less recognition of the charm to be found amongst some of the lesser-known species.

Some clematis produce a mass of small flowers whilst others display huge, exotic blooms which can be 8in (20cm) in diameter. The colours cover most of the spectrum with whites, pinks and reds, although the preponderant hues are in the purple, violet and mauve range. Colour is very

much a personal interpretation, but it would be accurate to say that there are few true reds and no pure blues because clematis flowers are usually subtle blends of pigment. The appearance is, therefore, more maroon than scarlet and although the vivid blue of gentian, for instance, is not represented in clematis, every shade around this part of the spectrum is superbly evident. Amongst the most popular hybrids which are available nowadays are those which have flowers with contrasting bands of colour.

Clematis have received considerable attention from the plant breeders and, as a consequence, different hybrids vary in their constitution, vigour and hardiness. Yet apart from some tender species, the bulk can confidently be classed as hardy. Freezing conditions over long periods are tolerated by plants which are dormant, and although precocious growth which occurs early in the year can be damaged, any dieback is usually temporary and the plants are not unduly troubled by such set-backs.

The cultivation of clematis is largely simple and trouble free, and although pruning does provoke some apprehension, it is really a straightforward procedure. As with most permanent garden subjects, it is prudent to pay attention to soil preparation and the planting process, but, once established, clematis will prosper for decades. Naturally the best results will only be achieved by regular maintenance but this is uncomplicated and surely nobody would begrudge a modicum of effort in exchange for generations of beautiful displays. Clematis is widely known as the 'Queen of Climbers' but this should not convey the idea of a plant which demands special treatment or sophisticated support. Newcomers to the cultivation of these plants will soon recognize the regal qualities and will become enthusiastic about providing the support and sustenance which all monarchs require.

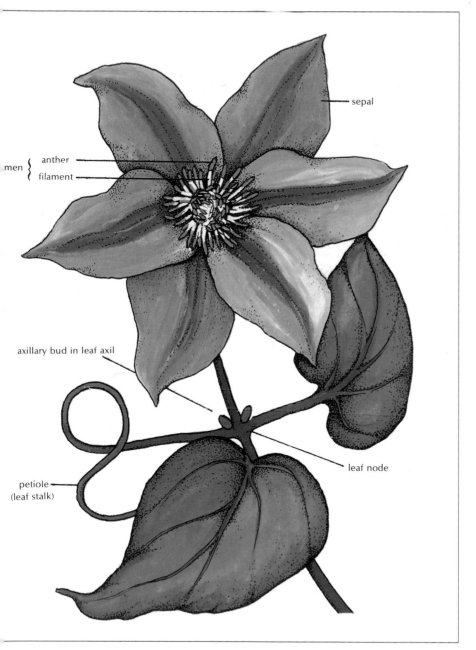

sepal

men { anther
    { filament

axillary bud in leaf axil

leaf node

petiole
(leaf stalk)

~ parts of a clematis.

1 • PLANTING

Virtually any soil will be adequate for growing clematis but any plant which offers such great pleasure over many decades deserves some initial effort. Reasonable results are almost guaranteed, but most gardeners will want to see a good performance and many will set themselves the challenge of achieving the best. The plant's position in the garden is undoubtedly an important consideration but of paramount concern is the soil.

Soil

Inexperienced cultivators may believe that the material in which plants grow is just soil but there are various kinds of soils and there is an enormous range of quality. The supply of nutrients seems to be a current preoccupation, but the most vital characteristic of a good growing medium is its ability to retain moisture without becoming waterlogged.

Where a garden has been cultivated over a number of years, the soil will have been considerably improved. Even without human measures, this will have been effected by the natural processes of rain and frost, and the essential component of humus will have been added by decaying leaves and other organic material. However, this process is slow and it may not be sufficiently advanced to enable plants to thrive.

Recently constructed houses often have gardens which present obstacles to cultivation, usually in the form of builders' rubble, pockets of sand or concrete, or, at best, heavily compacted ground. Wholesale clearance of underground rubbish can be a daunting task and many gardeners prefer the option of piecemeal improvement where planting is to take place. Whatever the situation, the identification of good soil may be difficult for the inexperienced and I would therefore advise the following

C. viticella   This is a southern European species whose flowers do not enrapture everyone but whose sheer profusion and extended period of display are ample compensations. There are several varieties, the most acclaimed of which are 'Etoile Violette', 'Royal Velours' and the double-flowered 'Purpurea Plena Elegans'.

routine procedures, especially when plan[ ]ing long-term subjects like clematis.

Site Preparation

Ideally, the planting station should be exc[ ]vated 18in (46cm) square and the sam[ ]depth. If the soil is reasonable, it c[ ]be mixed with a generous quantity of pe[ ]The use of this material for horticulture h[ ]become an emotive subject, but fortunate[ ]there are effective substitutes for the purpo[ ]

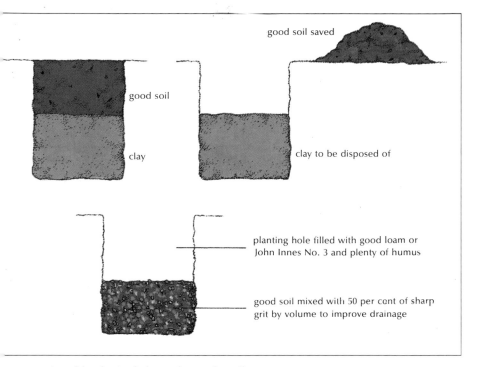

good soil saved

good soil

clay

clay to be disposed of

planting hole filled with good loam or
John Innes No. 3 and plenty of humus

good soil mixed with 50 per cent of sharp
grit by volume to improve drainage

e preparation of the planting hole on a heavy clay soil.

soil improvement. Well-composted gar-
n waste is excellent and so, too, is leaf
ould; rotted farmyard or stable manure is
e classic option, but nowadays local sup-
es are rarely encountered except in rural
eas. The other recommended ingredient
a planting mix is a spadeful of sharp sand
grit which will assist in draining the root
n.

The main danger, which might be
countered, is a very heavy clay subsoil
d, without suitable treatment, it would be
death trap for clematis and most other
ants whose roots would inevitably
come waterlogged. There is no con-
diction in the requirement of a moisture-
entive soil and avoiding excess water –
nt roots require air to remain healthy
d this is excluded when excess water is

present. Complete removal of the clay or
the incorporation of large quantities of
organic matter are the only solutions and, in
extreme cases, it might be necessary to use
artificial means of drainage. Another problem may occur when a planting site next to
a house wall is chosen because this is often
rubble-ridden and impoverished. The only
viable course of action is to remove as
much of the poor soil as possible and
replace it, either with soil from elsewhere or
with a bag of John Innes potting compost
from the garden centre.

When the hole has been dug, the soil at
the bottom should be broken up before
some rotted compost is added. On top of
that, about 12in (30cm) of soil and peat mix
needs to be added and gently firmed; this
should then be sprinkled with a handful of

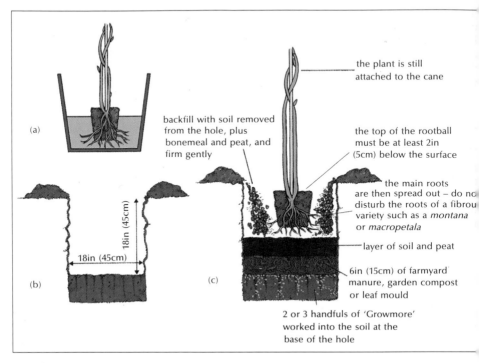

Planting clematis. (a) If the clematis is at all dry, soak it in water for 10–20 minutes. (b) Dig a hole 18in (45cm) square and deep, and fork the soil at the bottom and sides to loosen it. (c) Prepare the nutrients to provide nourishment for the plant once it is established. If the surrounding soil is dry, the plant should be watered in.

bonemeal which is a long-lasting, natural fertilizer. At this point, the young plant can be positioned in the hole to ascertain the depth of planting. It is important to ensure that the top of the rootball will be 4–6in (10–15cm) below ground level. This depth will enable the buried stem to grow additional roots and also to promote renewal shoots in the future.

Container Plants

The vast majority of clematis are sold as container plants; that is, they are in the pots in which they have grown, and a short cane is invariably used for supporting the stem. This is certainly the best way to buy them and although some open-rooted plants may be found, I would not advise anyone to buy these. They may be a little cheaper, but clematis are resentful of root disturbance and open-rooted plants are slower to establish and can fail completely. Container plants have a firm rootball which has been moulded by the pot and, consequently, they can be located in the planting hole with the minimum of disruption.

It is widely acknowledged that container-grown plants will become established more quickly if some of the major roots are teased apart and spaced out in the planting position.

However, I believe it is more convenient and advantageous for the inexperienced if the roots are undisturbed. This is certainly true for many species and small-flowered clematis whose roots are essentially fibrous and more likely to suffer damage.

Location

One further point is worth mentioning for those clematis which will spend their lives growing against house walls. It is prudent to position the plant so that the rootball is at least 12in (30cm) from the wall with the cane inserted at an angle towards the

Most clematis are sold in containers.

'Jackmanii' This is probably the most famous of all clematis and was bred by George Jackman and Son in Woking. It flowered for the first time in 1862. It is the variety which began the huge interest in hybrids. The purple blooms are quite large and are produced *en masse* from June onwards.

support framework. This practice avoids exposing the roots to the very dry soil which is typical of this location, often made worse where an overhanging roof or gutter prevents rain from falling on the ground underneath.

Finishing Touches

Having placed the clematis in its final position, the remaining soil is replaced and firmed by gentle treading, preferably to a

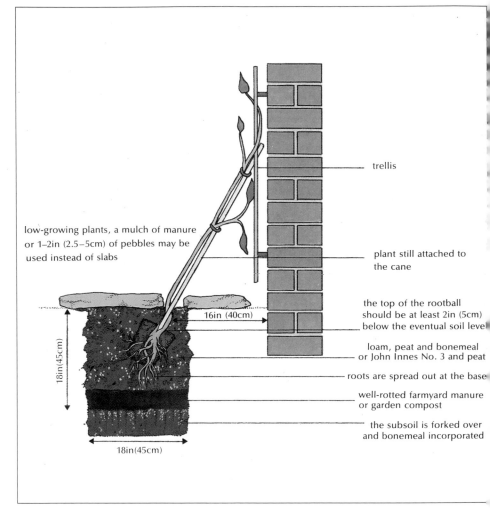

low-growing plants, a mulch of manure
or 1–2in (2.5–5cm) of pebbles may be
used instead of slabs

16in (40cm)

18in(45cm)

18in(45cm)

trellis

plant still attached to
the cane

the top of the rootball
should be at least 2in (5cm)
below the eventual soil level

loam, peat and bonemeal
or John Innes No. 3 and peat

roots are spread out at the base

well-rotted farmyard manure
or garden compost

the subsoil is forked over
and bonemeal incorporated

The method for planting clematis against a wall.

slightly lower level than the surrounding
ground. This slight hollow will facilitate
effective use of the watering-can which
is the final act of planting. It should be
stressed that the advice given in this chapter
is of the utmost significance, because the
measures taken during planting are the most
influential for the future. If your intention is

to plant more than one clematis, there will
be an understandable reluctance to dig out
3½ cu ft (1 cu m) for each plant; indeed, it
may not be possible for every location.
However, the investment of time and effort
will pay dividends for years to come. May I
remind you of the oft-quoted phrase – plant
in haste, regret at leisure.

2 • AFTERCARE AND CULTIVATION

Container plants are usually available throughout the year and may be planted at any time provided that the soil is neither frozen nor very wet. Nevertheless, autumn and spring are the traditional and best seasons for planting and anyone dealing with specialist clematis nurseries will find that their plants are ready for sale before the autumn arrives. After the first generous watering, it is wise to place a piece of paving stone over the rooting area in order to provide some shade and hence some protection from drying out.

Watering

The first year in the garden life of any plant is crucial. It needs to form a good network of roots and build up a constitution to overcome the inevitable climatic set-backs of the future. Remembering that clematis are moisture lovers, supplementary water-ing will probably be necessary, especially if the first summer after planting is long and hot. Thereafter, these climbers should be virtually independent, although there are some requirements which should be met annually and, when possible, the plants may need to be assisted during drought conditions.

Feeding

Farmyard manure is a rare commodity, but, where it can be obtained, there are few materials which are better for using than a mulch. Mulching is the process of spread-ing a 1–2in (2.5–5cm) layer over the root zone which will reduce the evaporation of moisture, suppress weed growth and, if possible, provide a gradual supply of nutrients. Manure satisfies these needs per-fectly but there are many substitutes, such as garden compost, leaf mould, bark chippings

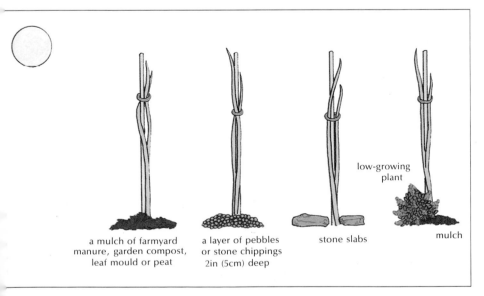

a mulch of farmyard manure, garden compost, leaf mould or peat

a layer of pebbles or stone chippings 2in (5cm) deep

stone slabs

low-growing plant

mulch

There are several different methods of shading the roots to keep them cool. The areas covered should be about 20in (50cm) in diameter.

Flowers with contrasting bands of colour are especially popular – 'Bee's Jubilee'.

'Etoile Violette' (C. viticella) is suitable for any aspect.

nd even well-rotted grass cuttings, which
nly require a modest supplement of a
eneral fertilizer.

Clematis which are inadequately sup-
lied with moisture and plant food will
roduce progressively smaller flowers.
hose varieties which have a second flush
f bloom later in the season are particularly
 need of regular feeding. In early spring,
t the same time as applying the mulch, a
ood handful of bonemeal, blood, fish and
one mixture or the fertilizer 'Growmore',
ould be sprinkled around the plant. These
re all available as powder or granules and
is dry state means that the nutrients are
pplied to the plant over a long period,
eing gradually dissolved by rainfall. The
ternative, which entails more effort, is a
quid feed watered in every three weeks or
 during the growing season. Liquid ferti-
zers act very quickly and it is worth bear-
g in mind that as well as being applied to
e soil, they can be sprayed onto the
liage for an even quicker effect.

nnual Maintenance

here are many people who go through
eir gardening lives with the minimum of
fort whilst achieving agreeable and admir-
le results, but unless you believe yourself
 be one of the blessed, then basic precau-
ons are unavoidable. In some instances,
ematis have been planted with little fuss
d merely the expedient of making a small
le in the soil, but this technique leaves
ccess in the lap of the gods. Ignoring the
nnual maintenance is common, especially
nongst those whose interests lie in display
ther than gardening, and it often goes
punished, but it is an uncertain path to
llow. The routines are neither arduous nor
pensive and even a small amount of
nely attention will bring handsome
turns.

Every specimen plant in the garden

'Nelly Moser' A great many gardeners who
do not grow clematis are, nevertheless,
familiar with this name as it has been a
favourite since its introduction in 1897. The
sepals are a subtle pink/mauve with a central
band in lilac/pink but both colours fade very
badly in strong sunlight. In shade or semi-
shade, it looks magnificent.

benefits from regular observation so that
cultural deficiencies can be detected at an
early stage and rectified. Lack of vigour is
usually caused by water or nutrient shortage,
or both. An otherwise healthy plant which
flowers spasmodically – or rarely – is probably exposed to an excess of nitrogen in the
soil and to insufficient potash. Unenthusiastic
growers may view such detail as irksome, but
maintenance is the essence of cultivation.

Of course, there are those gardeners who
enjoy the process of plant care and they will
find that clematis reward them amply as a
responsive and highly decorative subject.

3 • SITE AND SUPPORT

The native habitat of any plant gives valuable clues to the conditions which it prefers and, if we can duplicate them in our gardens, the likelihood of its prosperity is greatly enhanced. Clematis belong to the hedgerows and light woodland with their roots shaded and their stems clinging as they climb into the sunlight. Leaf litter and the proximity of other plants give the protection which conserves soil moisture, and the decomposition of leaves provides nutrition. The climbing is accomplished by twisting leaf stalks around the twigs and branches of trees and shrubs, and no harm is caused to the hosts. This support is essential, not only because it enables

'Comtesse de Bouchaud' thrives in most positions.

Florida *'Sieboldii' should be grown against a sheltered wall to minimize weather damage.*

clematis to climb, but also because gives shelter from damaging winds – th additional requirement must be met in th garden situation.

Every garden deserves a clematis and having decided to grow one or more, th best plan is to identify the sites which a ideal or nearly so. Alternatively, it shou be determined where clematis would b desirable to cover an eyesore or decora an unoccupied spot. The vast majority climbers are grown up house walls and th surely stems from a desire to provic interest and colour where there is only pla

ickwork. Most dwellings have paths
ound them and, in parts at least, these
ill be right up against the walls. Clearly,
is makes the provision of cultivated
itches rather difficult but if it is decided to
eak through the concrete or remove pav-
g stones, there is the compensation of
owing that these sites are excellent for
ematis. Their roots will spread under the
ived area and benefit from the coolness
id inherent moisture retention. Growing
ese plants against a house will not have
ifortunate repercussions for the building
cause although some varieties are vigor-
is, their roots are not capable of causing
image to the foundations.

orth, South, East or West?

long as there is reasonably good light, a
great many clematis varieties will thrive,
even if little direct sunshine falls on the
location. This gives the opportunity to
clothe walls which are unsuitable for most
flowering plants. The widespread belief that
a southern aspect is best for all is an over-
simplification and quite inaccurate for some
clematis.

Firstly, it must be recognized that the
conditions which prevail in sunny and
warm climates are enormously different
from those in less hospitable localities, and
gardeners will have to make judgements
based on their own knowledge. A north-
facing wall in cold and exposed areas
would not allow many clematis to flourish
and this is especially true of the large-
flowered hybrids; probably only the *alpina,
macropetala* and *montana* types would be
suitable. Less extreme climates will allow a
wider range of clematis to perform well,

e President', whose flowers prosper in sun or shade.

including some of the large-flowering kinds.

A southern wall is certainly appropriate for most clematis but it does pose the problem of very dry soil caused by the brickwork absorbing moisture and sunshine causing rapid evaporation. If a southern aspect is chosen, it may be necessary to water a plant copiously when rainfall is scarce and I should warn that even average rainfall may not be sufficient to sustain clematis in peak condition during the summer.

Another consideration, apart from the well-being of the plant, is that of flower colour, and there are some general guide-

lines which are relevant in this respect. Re flowers and most blue ones need dire sunshine to bring out the colour proper but some of those with more delicate hue will fade very badly if they are not grown i comparative shade.

Having highlighted the problems c northerly and southerly aspects, it can b said that east and west are most likely t be conducive to success with clematis. Th local climate will have a great influence, c course, but usually east and west will affor a good balance between sunshine an shade with the consequent protection fro undue moisture loss. Perhaps the exceptic to this rule is an easterly aspect in col regions where winter and early sprir winds can cause damage to those shoc which emerge first. Having said that, tr clematis is a resilient plant and it is high unlikely that slight damage will have ar significant effect on the season's flowerir performance.

Fences

The problem of dry soil next to house wa is not a consideration in the garden itself b it would still be prudent to take the utmc care in preparing the planting site. Waterir during the first year is a priority, too, b subsequently clematis will be perfectly se sufficient and although the best results v come from annual mulching and feedir plants in the garden will be better able resist neglect.

Perhaps the only limitation imposed c fence-grown clematis is the actual height the structure. Very few, if any, varieties v be confined happily to less than 6ft (2n which is somewhat taller than the avera boundary fence. This does not invalida the planting of clematis under these c cumstances, but it does mean that tr shoots will need to be trained horizonta to some extent and tied to supporting wire

'Ernest Markham' This is another famous name in clematis culture. Ernest Markham raised many hybrids but the one which bears his name is widely acknowledged to be the best red of them all. It is a late-flowering plant which must be grown in a sunny position for the best results.

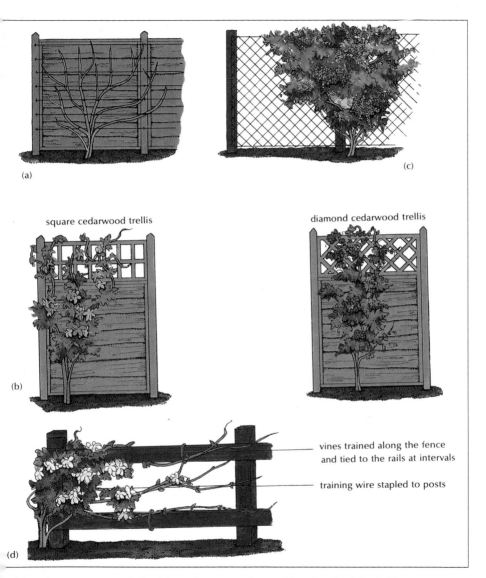

(a)

(c)

square cedarwood trellis

diamond cedarwood trellis

(b)

vines trained along the fence
and tied to the rails at intervals

training wire stapled to posts

(d)

raining wires are necessary for larch lap or interwoven fences. The wires should be held away
om the fence panels to allow the clematis to twine around them. (b) The maximum height for
ost fencing panels is 6ft (2m). There are many clematis in the 6–9ft (2–3m) range which are
itable, and extra height can be achieved by using longer posts and a trellis extension. (c) An
sightly chain-link fence can be obscured by a montana or other vigorous species variety.
) The flowers of some varieties, such as 'Marie Boisselot' and 'Lord Nevill', are held
rizontally. They are ideally suited to being trained along a low fence where they can be
ewed from above.

Tall-growing, hard-pruning varieties that have an abundance of flower at the top are ideally suited to supports that need to be clothed well above ground level. (a) Simple metal or rustic arches. (b) Open rustic screens spanning the garden.

Posts and Pergolas

House walls and fences are existing structures which can support climbers but keen
gardeners will want to construct 'flower tow-
ers'. These can take the form of traditional
pergolas and colonnades but there are other
ways of achieving the same end. Single
posts with lengths of wire between are one
option and wigwam shapes can be erected
which comprise a central post with wires
taken from the top and attached to strong
pegs in the ground. Wherever posts are
used, it must be remembered that a full
canopy of clematis foliage offers considerable wind resistance and, therefore, they
must be erected very stoutly. Typically, this
will entail 8ft (2.5m) above ground with
about 18in (46cm) set in concrete.

Obviously, there is some effort involved
with all of these structures, but I would offer
the opinion that columns of bloom add an

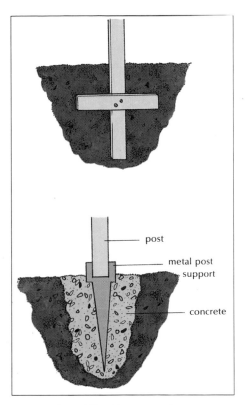

post

metal post
support

concrete

*Posts can be stabilized by means of a
horizontal piece of wood nailed on below
ground level, or, if more strength is
required, metal post supports can be
purchased.*

interesting upright dimension to the garden
and the effect is magnificent.

Natural Planting

A clematis that is able to follow its natural
inclination by scrambling through shrubs and
trees is unquestionably a glorious sight but
not without its difficulties. Like all 'natural'
planting in the confines of a domestic garden, it requires some forethought if the
enterprise is to be worth while. In large

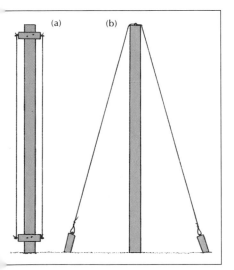

(a)   (b)

*(a) Wires attached to small blocks of wood
nailed to the top and bottom of the post.
(b) Wires stapled to the top of the post are
taken down and attached to pegs driven
into the ground, giving a triangular structure.*

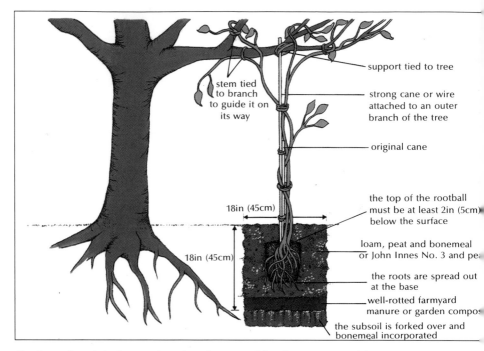

Planting a clematis to the outer branches of a tree avoiding the tree roots and the canopy.

gardens, which have a shrubbery or wooded area, suitable host plants may be plentiful but the size and formality of normal gardens imposes restrictions.

Trees with dense canopies will be too dark, and mature specimens with large and smooth trunks make it impossible for clematis to cling effectively; also the attachment of netting, for instance, may not be aesthetically pleasing for some gardeners. The alternative is to plant some distance from the trunk and underneath a suitable branch; a vertical stake can then be fixed in the ground and secured to the branch. The lower growth will need to be tied to the stake but once the leading shoots have reached the branch, they can ramble to good purpose.

Where shrubs are used as clematis supports, some account must be taken of the

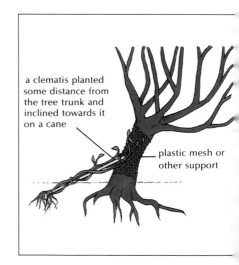

Clematis planted against the trunk of a tree that does not have a large canopy.

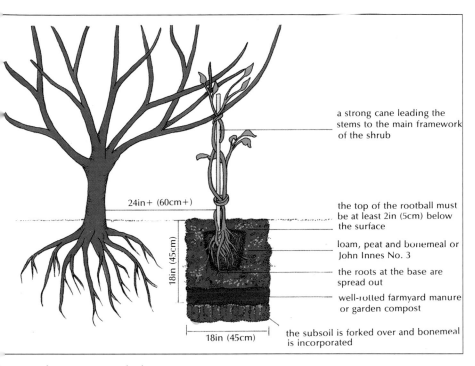

a strong cane leading the stems to the main framework of the shrub

24in+ (60cm+)

18in (45cm)

the top of the rootball must be at least 2in (5cm) below the surface

loam, peat and bonemeal or John Innes No. 3

the roots at the base are spread out

well-rotted farmyard manure or garden compost

18in (45cm)

the subsoil is forked over and bonemeal is incorporated

anting a clematis against a shrub.

corative value of the host candidates. A ature forsythia or mock orange can be eal because both of these popular plants e most attractive in their season but there- er are notably dull. When a forsythia, for stance, has finished flowering at the end April its firm but quite open network of anches makes an excellent support for a splay of clematis in the summer. It does ghtly complicate the business of pruning, t only to the extent that some secateur ork may be needed on the forsythia – this ould be carried out in May.

The choice of appropriate varieties of matis is important for all locations, but ore so when they are incorporated into an en garden plan. If evergreens are used as sts, it would not be pleasing to have their nter profile spoiled by a profusion of brown clematis stems and, in this case, it is advisable to plant those varieties which are pruned hard each year. Although the general advice is to prune such clematis in spring, there is no good reason why it should not be done in November, thereby removing the offending growth before it becomes prominent.

One other effective plan is to train clematis horizontally in a bed and in this case it is necessary to choose a clematis which is more or less continuously in flower. Quite a large bed will be required because suitable varieties tend to be rather vigorous and I have seen very few small gardens using this technique; it is, however, possible to achieve unusual and spectacular results. It is desirable to provide some means of keeping the growth a little above ground level or

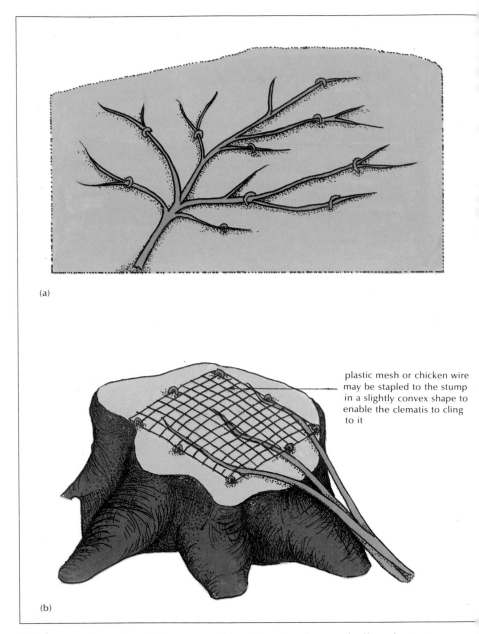

(a)

(b)

plastic mesh or chicken wire
may be stapled to the stump
in a slightly convex shape to
enable the clematis to cling
to it

(a) A young montana, *the main stems pegged down to create a framework of branches on a sloping bank. (b) A young* alpina *or* macropetala *planted against a tree stump. The support mesh will quickly be covered by a framework of stems.*

e blooms will become splashed with soil
uring heavy rainfall, but this is easily
ccomplished with short posts and netting.
therwise, clematis can be allowed to ram-
le over rockeries with the main growth
egged at suitable intervals.

upport Systems

should be emphasized that clematis are
ole to cling by means of leaf stems which
rap themselves around objects which are
f a convenient size. There is no prospect of
lants securing themselves to brick walls or
nces and so it is essential to attach netting,
ires or a wooden trellis.

The trellis has an acceptably traditional

'Comtesse de Bouchaud' Although bred just
after the turn of the twentieth century, this
remains one of the most popular clematis,
producing masses of rose-pink blooms over
most of the summer. Its vigorous nature
makes it ideal for covering large walls.

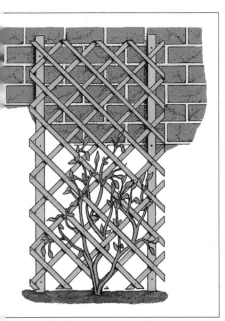

ooden trellis fixed to the wall by means
vertical laths of wood. This allows
ace between the trellis and the wall to
able the stems and petioles to twine
ht round the support.

look and is favoured by many, but it needs
to be fixed in such a way that there is space
between the trellis and the wall. This is
facilitated by plugging the wall, screwing
battens to it, and then screwing the trellis to
the battens. Screws are preferable to nails
because, at some time, the trellis will be
removed for maintenance (the application
of a wood preservative, for example). If
creosote is used, the work must be com-
pleted in early winter because this sub-
stance is highly corrosive and will certainly
scorch the leaves and stems. After five or six
weeks, the fumes will have dispersed but I
must say that I prefer using preservatives

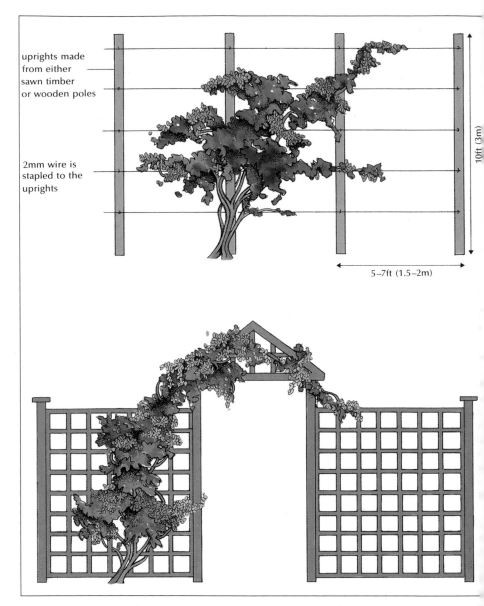

uprights made
from either
sawn timber
or wooden poles

2mm wire is
stapled to the
uprights

10ft (3m)

5–7ft (1.5–2m)

A vertical post sunk into the ground and joined by horizontal wires quickly makes an effective and dense screen when planted with the varieties of vigorous species such as serratifolia, tangutica *and* rehderiana. *Ready-made trellis sections can be made into appropriately sized screens, in various designs to make individual supports for clematis.*

*o facilitate maintenance on a rendered or
ainted surface, plastic-coated clematis
ellis can be attached to the wall by
neans of large hooks, enabling the whole
ing to be lifted down.*

which are not harmful to vegetation.

Rigid plastic netting is the most versatile
upport and while it can be stapled to
wooden battens, it is also possible to sus-
end it on hooks and this enables the
etting to be lifted off most conveniently.
Although strong and fairly rigid, it can also
e curved around posts and pergolas and, if
dequately staked, it can be fixed to short
osts to support ground-cover plants. It is
so readily wrapped around tree trunks.

The wigwam frames which are made
pecifically for climbing plants can be used
s centre-pieces on lawns and are con-
tructed from plastic-coated metal rods
which are pushed into the soil. They can
so stand in large tubs making the support
f container clematis much easier than with
ther methods.

Less specialized forms of support can be
tilized, such as stout wires fixed at intervals

to posts and on walls, but in the latter case,
some vertical wires are desirable to assist
climbing shoots. The wires can be fixed to
fittings called vine eyes and this system is
inexpensive and convenient for large areas,
although it may look rather sparse until the
clematis has established its framework.
Wherever wires are used instead of trellis
or netting, some tying with soft string is
advisable.

The success of any support system
depends on strong materials and firm fixing,
as even a relatively small clematis, in full
leaf, is quite heavy and at the mercy of the
winds. In very exposed areas, it would be
sensible to confine clematis cultivation to
the shelter of walls and stout fences and
avoid the free-standing structures.

Since gardens are designed for the ornamental display of plants, I appreciate the
opinion that all support measures are ob-
trusive. However, unless there are oppor-
tunities to utilize natural supports, it is
inevitable that nets, wires and posts will be
visible for part of the year. If this is
unacceptable, I strongly suggest that extra
thought is given to systems which have
minimum visual impact, or to those that can
be dismantled for the close season. Remov-
able netting has been mentioned, but it is
quite possible to devise a garden plan that
allows other plants to camouflage the
offending structures, perhaps by growing
some evergreen subjects in strategic situa-
tions. Individual posts and pillars pose a
greater problem, and they can certainly
look gaunt and bleak when they are not
clothed with foliage. Nevertheless, a visit to
a good garden centre or hardware super-
market will reveal more options than might
be expected. For instance, there are post
holders which, set in the ground, allow a
firm footing for inserting either metal or
wooden posts, and allow simple removal of
posts for the winter.

4 • CLEMATIS IN TUBS

There is an increasing interest in plant containers because they add considerably to the decorative potential of terraces and other paved areas and, within limits, they enable gardeners to move a display for the best effect. Clematis, like most other plants, are perfectly suited to life in large tubs with the proviso that the less vigorous varieties are chosen. Those which have the potential to grow 40ft (12m) high will not be happily restricted in a container, but compact plants can be managed very well. This means that most of the large-flowered hybrids will do reasonably well with proper attention, but there are some varieties which can excel.

Containers

Large tubs are preferable, in other words, 18–20in (46–50cm) in diameter and equally deep, but the material used in their construction affects the cost and the suitability for planting. Half-barrels are the most characterful and wood is light compared to its strength, but just as useful is the fact that it is a good insulator against extremes of temperature. It does need periodic maintenance and removing the plant for this purpose may become an irksome task, but the application of preservative is quick and simple.

Reconstituted stone is a good-looking compromise bearing in mind the prohibitive cost of the real thing, and is more attractive than concrete. Both are very heavy, but they are maintenance-free and will last for generations.

Plastic has the advantage of lightweight strength but even if it has been ultraviolet stabilized, it will become brittle with age and will eventually crack and disintegrate. Fibreglass is equally light and can last indefinitely, being immune to cracking and splitting, and some are designed as reproductions of stone tubs in various styles. Unfortunately, however, fibreglass is quite expensive.

Cultivation

The first essential requirement is a good compost, and in this instance a peat-based medium is not as satisfactory as that based on loam. John Innes compost is not as common as it used to be, but it is sold by most garden centres and the No. 3 formula is best for our purpose because it contains the highest level of nutrients. Nevertheless, annual top-dressing will be essential to sustain adequate growth and this is accomplished by removing the top 2in (5cm) of old compost and replacing with fresh material. In addition, container-grown plants will need regular feeding throughout the growing season with either solid or liquid fertilizers.

It is also most important to ensure that the compost drains freely, and after checking that there are sufficient holes in the base of the tub, these should be covered with a 1in (2.5cm) layer of stones or broken crocks. I would recommend that the container sit on old tiles so that the drainage holes are slightly above ground level and will not become clogged by an accumulation of debris.

Location

The use of a container will enable a clematis to be grown up a house wall in places where access to the soil is prevented and, in this case, a conventional support system can be used as outlined in Chapter 3. If, on the other hand, the intention is to decorate somewhere away from walls or other vertical structures, then some integral system must be employed. One arrangement consists of four strong canes pushed into the compost, around which is placed a section of semi-rigid netting tied securely with string. If the growing shoots are trained to spiral around the support framework, the result will be considerably more compact

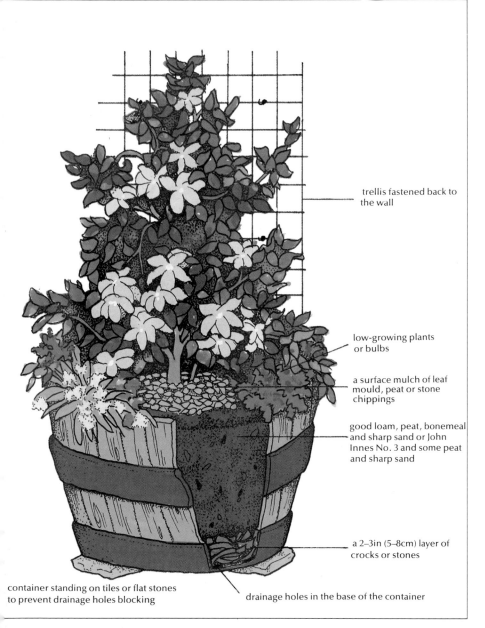

trellis fastened back to
the wall

low-growing plants
or bulbs

a surface mulch of leaf
mould, peat or stone
chippings

good loam, peat, bonemeal
and sharp sand or John
Innes No. 3 and some peat
and sharp sand

a 2–3in (5–8cm) layer of
crocks or stones

container standing on tiles or flat stones
to prevent drainage holes blocking

drainage holes in the base of the container

large container may be planted with low-growing subjects as well as the clematis. Good
rainage is essential.

Spiral form of training to produce a compact plant.

during the summer and, even when rainfall seems plentiful, it is unlikely that the tub will not need the attentions of a watering can at least every other day. The canopy of leaves will completely overhang the container which means that very little rain will reach the compost. Even if this were not so a growing clematis in full leaf and in warm dry weather may actually use 1 gallon (4.5 litres) of water each day and neglect may lead to dehydration.

The other major obstacle to success with tubs is the danger of severe winter weather. A container affords little protection to the roots during prolonged, freezing conditions and damage can ensue. If the plant is climbing up wall-mounted supports and cannot be moved, the only remedy is to use a mound of peat or soil to cover the tub completely. Containers that can be moved are easily overwintered in a sheltered part of the garden or even partially buried. Mobile plants are the best because, not only can they be given temporary protection they can also occupy favoured positions whilst in flower. This means that a collection of clematis can be displayed prominently whilst blooming and relegated to a unseen site at other times. If you are attracted by the idea of a mobile display then I would recommend that you purchase a two-wheeled trolley, designed like those used by railway porters, so that the deployment of tubs is not an arduous chore.

Suitable Varieties

The general advice is to select from those clematis which are not unduly vigorous and those which can be expected to perform satisfactorily are mentioned at the end of this book (*see* page 59). The late flowering hybrids are mostly rather tall whereas the *alpina* and *macropetala* are more diminutive and especially good with restricted root space.

than with free-growing plants. It requires frequent attention as growth ensues but the ultimate effect of a 5–6ft (1.5–1.8m) clematis, literally covered in bloom, is really outstanding. Of course, plants grown in this way must be sheltered from strong winds and there are some drawbacks to having clematis in tubs.

Remembering that clematis are moisture lovers, regular watering is a prerequisite

5 • PRUNING

Without doubt this is a word which strikes fear in the hearts of gardeners, novice and experienced alike, and it is the subject of myth and mystery. Plants thrived on this planet for millions of years before the advent of secateurs and, therefore, some question the necessity for pruning. Actually, vegetation was 'pruned' — by browsing animals, lightning, strong winds and disease. Fortunately for the plants, the vast majority have the capacity, not only to survive damage, but also to regenerate and effectively replace what has been lost.

In the garden, pruning is often undertaken to remove damaged stems but this human intervention is not usually essential to the plant's survival. This kind of pruning is principally aesthetic, but where disease is evident the removal of affected parts will inhibit the malady from spreading. Another reason for cutting off some growth is simply to restrict the plant to its allotted space. This

The white inclined flowers of C. alpina *are always eye-catching and prolifically produced.*

'Vyvyan Pennell' A newer variety (1959) which is renowned for its double flowers, but it is really a dual-purpose plant. The double, soft purple flowers arrive in late spring but many growers prefer the single flowers which are a lighter shade and are displayed in September.

is entirely justified and often essential. If the specimen is becoming too large and beginning to intrude on its neighbours, it is right and proper to remove that which offends.

Both these reasons are applicable to clematis but there is one more factor which should be considered as an act of cultivation — pruning to optimize a plant's performance. Left alone, most garden subjects will thrive, but gardeners demand much more and perhaps I can use the example of hybrid tea roses to illustrate my point. It is

(a) A tall-growing, hard-pruning clematis with two winter pruning points. (b) The new vines are later trained to provide an abundance of summer blooms.

ommonly accepted that roses should be
uned each spring although many who
llow the practice may not be aware of
hy they are doing it. Without fairly severe
duction in the length of old stems, the
sult would be a mass of tangled growth
id new shoots would only appear at the
p of the plant. A profusion of flowers
ould ensue but these would have little
dividual quality and in a surprisingly
ort space of time, the bush would age
id become unproductive. On the other
ind, frequent removal of old branches
ctually stimulates the renewal process,
juvenates the bush, prolongs active life,
id, most importantly, improves the
ooms.

With clematis, pruning may be needed
r other reasons, but the principal aim is
encourage a growing framework for
regular, large and high-quality flowers. The
main confusion is brought about by the fact
that different types flower at differing times
of the year and consequently pruning is not
the same for all. In past literature, clematis
have been grouped into categories accord-
ing to the various species from which they
derived but, especially where the large-
flowered hybrids are concerned, this is of
doubtful significance. Inter-breeding, over
many decades, has resulted in cultivars
which can hardly be attributed to parent
species and in many cases it would be
impossible to trace the family line. Names
like *lanuginosa* and *patens* are not encountered except in old books and, other than
for those interested in the history of clematis, these species have no relevance to the
modern gardener. What is much more per-
tinent, for pruning purposes, is how and

viticella *Etoile Violette is happy rambling over other plants in the shrub border.*

'Ville de Lyon', a variety which needs sunshine for the best results.

'Lambton Park' (C. tangutica) has medium flowers and large seedheads.

hen clematis flower, and I hope that the
llowing explanation puts pruning into its
roper context.

Many plants grow stems and then flower
n the current year's growth; others make
owth in one year which then supports
owers in the following year; some plants
o a bit of both. Inconveniently, clematis
e represented in each of these groups and
ence there are three headings for consider-
ion. This technicality does not make the
sk more difficult, but only requires know-
dge of the flowering period or the name of
e variety. In the plant list near the end of
is book (*see* page 53), each clematis vari-
y has one, or sometimes two, letters
hich indicate the pruning technique and

timing, and this practice is also followed in
the catalogues of specialist nurseries.

H – Hard

Those clematis which only flower after the
middle of June produce their blooms on
new wood which has grown in the current
year. Hence the whole of last year's stems
are redundant and should be removed in
the early spring. This will normally entail
cutting about 12–18in (30–46cm) above
soil level, ideally just above a pair of buds
which should be visible early in the year.
Guidance as to the timing of the operation
can only be vague, but usually it is in late

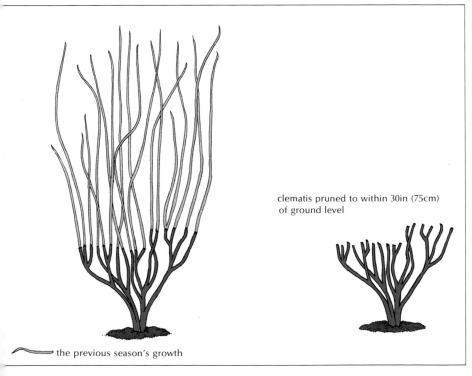

clematis pruned to within 30in (75cm)
of ground level

the previous season's growth

roup 3 clematis flower on the new season's growth. The old vines are removed by cutting
ck to a strong pair of buds. This group is referred to as H (hard).

year one

stems that are to
be pruned back

year two

The large-flowered mid-season varieties such as 'Henryi' and 'Marie Boisselot' can become very leggy if they are continually pruned only lightly. Reducing some stems to 30in (75cm) from ground level on alternate years will result in a plant that is well furnished at the base. Stems must only be cut back to a point just above two buds.

February or the beginning of March. Earlier pruning will promote new growth which may be damaged by frost and the decision will depend on local weather conditions.

If the plant is many years old, this annual pruning will lead to the formation of a large clump of woody material at the base, but it will be found that new shoots will emerge from the stump and often from beneath the soil. One situation which does provoke indecision is when the gardener is faced by new shoots which are quite advanced when pruning is timely. If the winter has been fairly mild, clematis may begin growing in January but the removal of some precocious shoots will not be detrimental to the plant and is essential if an organized and well-spaced framework is to be encouraged.

O – Optional

Species and cultivars which are spring flowering do not require pruning on a regular basis, but my belief is that plants in this group benefit greatly from an occasional cut back. After some years, specimens can become too large for convenience or present a massed tangle which does not show to best advantage. Pruning should take place after flowering has finished so that new shoots can grow and ripen in late summer and autumn and be ready to bear blooms in the following year. Very old clematis do pose a problem in that mature wood will not always 'break'; that is, may not be able to regenerate by producing new shoots from the woody base. The belt-and

...iobe' flowers during midsummer.

...he pretty C. armandii *needs a sheltered position.*

braces technique is to cut some stems low down and some higher up the plant, but these early-flowering clematis will not normally object to hard pruning.

P – Partial

One group of clematis, which include those hybrids flowering in mid-season an

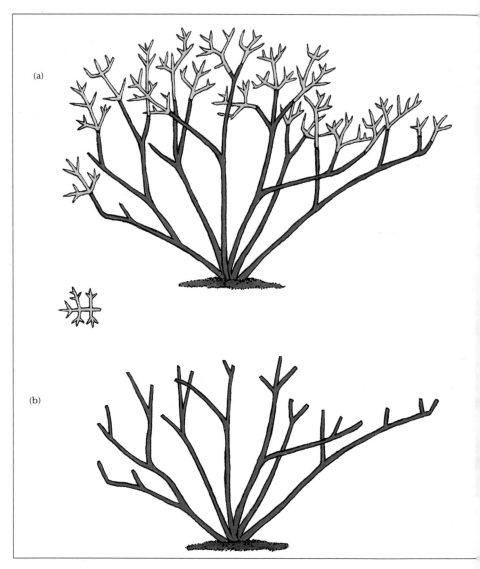

(a)

(b)

(a) Dead or weak stems (the previous year's flowering stems) cut back to a pair of fat buds. (b) Group 2 clematis after light pruning in February or early March. This group is referred to as P (partial).

me which flower earlier, does present
fficulties of choice because most will
wer on old and new shoots. The double-
d semi-double-flowered varieties usually
oom on the previous season's growth and
er in the year; they produce single
ooms on new shoots. The best treatment
to promote a permanent framework
nich comprises many mature stems and to
orten these each year. Occasionally, a
oportion of them can be cut back severely
stimulate new shoots and give options for
e future. The clematis which fall into this
tegory do constitute the majority of mod-
n hybrids but this should be construed as

C. flammula.

an opportunity to adopt a flexible approach
to pruning.

General Points

The first spring after planting, all clematis
should be pruned to the lowest pair of buds
and this action will prepare the groundwork
for all future training. If only one stem
grows in the following weeks, then the tip
must be pinched out so that a bushy multi-
stemmed plant is formed in the first year.

3arbara Jackman'   A most beautiful variety
om the famous Woking family with soft
nauve colouring overlaid with reddish-
urple bars. The bar colour does fade as the
owers age, but the creamy stamens make a
vely contrast.

'Wada's Primrose' – the nearest to yellow in the large-flowered varieties, it retains its colour if it is planted in a light but shady position.

From this time onwards, subsequent shoots can be spread out and loosely tied to supports so that growth occurs in the required direction.

There can be few doubts about pruning the 'hards' and the 'optionals' but whatever the prescribed procedure, it should be understood that incorrect pruning will not threaten the well-being of clematis. If, for example, spring-flowering plants are pruned early in the year they will still grow but much of the flowering potential will have been lost for one season. This will certainly be disappointing but such mistakes will not jeopardize the health of the plant. Where a clematis has been inherited by moving into another house and its name is not known, there will be uncertainty about the correct pruning. If it is allowed flower and the time of the season noted, will then be easy to place it into the rig category.

The rules of pruning are not hard and fa and should be adopted flexibly bearing mind the local weather conditions and t results which are required; this is necessa ily so with clematis in the 'partial' gro where some trial-and-error experience w be helpful. A light tidy-up is preferable recently planted varieties and thereafter combination of trimming and occasior severe pruning will be the most effecti strategy. Most important is to believe th pruning is a means of achieving your er with clematis. Errors will not have lor lasting effects.

• PESTS AND OTHER PROBLEMS

ll garden plants are subject to disease and sect attack but I am happy to relate that ematis are more trouble free than most, pecially if they are carefully nurtured ring the first two years of their lives. There ll be minor infringements by common sts and maybe some mildew, but only the lt disease will cause serious set-backs. nly the likely maladies are listed here.

phids

ese sap-feeding insects infest most plants t unless their numbers are great, clematis e well able to resist such attentions with-t repercussions. Attacks usually take ace in the very early spring when little e is available and it is the tips of new oots which are affected during mild ather. Leading shoots can be distorted by ge infestations and it is possible that me leaves will be malformed. A chemical sponse should not be automatic but rather ed as a last resort, because small birds d other insects feed on aphids and there ould be a reluctance to contaminate the od chain. A spray of soapy water, or nply wiping with a sponge or cloth, will fice but it is also possible to buy 'green' secticides which are specific in their ect and do not contain residues that are rmful to other wildlife.

aterpillars

leaves are seen which have been eaten ound the edges, the culprit will often be caterpillar of some moth or butterfly d, in the context of a large plant, the mage is quite insignificant. If there is ore injury than can be accepted, then I uld suggest a search-and-destroy mission her than a toxic spray, but remember that me plants must pay the price if we are to ve the beauty of butterflies and moths.

Earwigs

These armour-plated invaders are another seasonal threat and are normally active in the late summer and autumn when they eat parts of flowers. They favour dahlias and chrysanthemums but clematis are certainly on the menu and petals which have clearly been nibbled are a sure sign. Until about midsummer, earwigs eat other insects, including aphids, but thereafter they seem to become predominantly vegetarian. They often burrow into fairly mature flower buds and the pillage becomes evident only when the flowers open. Again, if the unfortunate effects are widespread, some action is indicated. Earwigs are very difficult to deter, but there are some chemicals which are at least partially effective. Upturned plant pots stuffed with straw or dried leaves will often lure earwigs into hiding and so too will half-sections of orange peel, but what to do with the captives is up to you.

Mice

For some gardeners, mice are a very serious clematis pest, eating all the buds which they can find, and it will almost certainly be necessary to use mousetraps to reduce the local population.

Slugs

Slugs are the worst enemy of the gardener. They will often take advantage of succulent shoots and though most damage is around ground level, they can, and will, climb walls and stems to reach green food. There is, in my view, no real alternative to using slug pellets but I should urge you to choose products for their minimal effect on other life. Tests have shown that properly consti-tuted pellets are not attractive to other animals and slugs that have succumbed are

'Royal Velours' is the deepest coloured of
the viticella.

their growth. If only a small proportion of
the plant is afflicted there will be no serious
complications, but a wholesale attack can
cause stems to die back. The first thing to do
is to remove all affected leaves and shoots
and burn them, then use a fungicide spray
over the whole plant. Clematis that have
shown themselves to be susceptible to mildew should be treated routinely, in early
summer, with a chemical which has systemic
action; that is, one which is absorbed by the
plant tissue, thereby protecting against
infection.

Wilt

Wilt is another fungus complaint, and one
which has achieved notoriety among clematis growers because of its truly dramatic
effects. A mature plant, or a major part of it,
can collapse quite suddenly without show-
ing any external symptoms of disease. For a
long time, the cause was believed to be cell
failure at periods of rapid growth, prevent-
ing the passage of water through the plant.
It is still thought that water blockage is to
blame but a fungus has been identified as
causing the cell to malfunction. Affected
parts must be removed and disposed of,
and what remains of the plant should be
thoroughly drenched with a fungicide. The
whole plant may wilt and, in this case,
will need to be cut right down to give it a
chance of recovery.

Clematis wilt is still a bit of a mystery, but
some factors have been pin-pointed;
attacks usually take place whilst the plant is
growing quickly, often just before flowering, and at times of high humidity. It has
also been convincingly demonstrated that
the plants which are best able to recover are
those which were planted deeply and thor-

most unlikely to be eaten by birds or other
creatures.

Mildew

Powdery mildew is a fungus that sometimes
afflicts clematis which are in a sheltered
position and have been subjected to dry
conditions. It is characterized by a powdery
deposit, usually seen first on leaves but
often spreading to shoots and inhibiting

*C. montana 'Rubens' is popular for masses
of clustered flowers.*

which received proper cultural attention during their early years. It is impossible to quantify the risk to individual clematis, but if it does occur in your garden, a fungicide should be used thereafter. Most clematis nurseries routinely spray their plants and drench the compost with benomyl. There is general confidence that this reduces the incidence of wilt.

The only other things to say about this frustrating ailment are that it rarely proves fatal and that it is more or less confined to the large-flowered hybrids; the pure species have not shown themselves to be at all susceptible. If a plant is struck down and cut back as far as possible, it will almost always regenerate. This can take a couple of years, however, so if it happens to your favourite climber, give it a chance to make a come-back first.

If a clematis is fatally afflicted, there is no reason why a new plant should not be put in the place from which the dead one has been removed. Careful growers may wish to replace most of the surrounding soil, but it should be remembered that wilt results from stem failure and not from root infection.

Miscellaneous Problems

One mishap which can overtake clematis is caused by household pets who get the idea that a prized climber is a fine place for a toilet. Quiet, sheltered locations make this likely and the final result will be the death of the clematis. Netting is one solution, but I think that such a sensitive matter is best resolved between the pet and his owner.

I must repeat that clematis is protected in nature by its host and this is especially true with wind. Young growth is very fragile and will be reduced to tatters if it is not properly secured. If gales coincide with cold weather, the prospects are worsened. Chill factor is recognized by human beings but it can also take its toll on fresh, tender foliage

which will turn brown as if it has been scorched. Frost, too, will take its toll of premature growth and, if severe, die-back is inevitable. However, the resilience of clematis will prompt renewed shoots and, unless freezing conditions prevail in late spring, successful blooming will not be jeopardized.

In some years, it has been found that the early-flowering varieties are disposed to produce flowers which are green, and this has been observed with Lasurstern and Nelly Moser, amongst others. If plants have received an annual application of a general fertilizer, this malady is unlikely to occur but, when it is encountered, a handful of sulphate of potash will restore normal colouring.

Reading a list of what might go wrong is rather daunting but it can be misleading. While your clematis may be affected by everything which has been mentioned, it is unlikely that they will suffer unduly. Life is full of ups and downs, even for the Queen of Climbers, but on balance it will come up smiling.

Perhaps one final point should be dealt with because it is fundamental to our purpose of growing decorative plants in the garden - failure to flower. A very severe winter can be the cause and so too can hard and incorrect pruning. If in doubt, do not prune at all during one year. This should enable you to determine the natural flowering time and, therefore, to adopt the best pruning programme for the future. Here, again, potash can be very helpful, and a regular feeding programme which includes a high proportion of potash will give an extra stimulus to the production of flowers. In the unlikely event of a continued absence of bloom, my advice is to dig up the offender and replace it. Like many flowering shrubs and trees, clematis may miss one year but any more than that is unpardonable. Life is too short to waste on the unfulfilled promise of beautiful flowers.

Those gardeners who have only just become acquainted with clematis will usually want to cement the relationship by cultivating the plants and there is no better way – to grow is definitely to know. When a passion develops, the desire is for additional information, and perhaps some detail about some propagation.

History

Clematis have been cultivated in European gardens since the latter part of the sixteenth century, but it was 200 years after that before they were given more than scant

'Lasurstern'   A moderately proportioned plant with lavender-blue blooms produced prolifically during late May and June with a late flush in September. Flower colour does fade in strong sunshine.

attention. Roses and tulips, for instance, had long been hybridized and otherwise improved in the quest for larger flowers, different colours and other desirable traits. Clematis activity never rivalled such flowers, but from 1850 until 1890 there was a procession of new hybrids, and catalogues of the time listed about 200 new varieties.

Initially, breeding was confined to species which originated in southern Europe, such as *alpina*, *cirrhosa*, *flammula*, *integrifolia* and *viticella*, and it is widely agreed that the last two were crossed to produce the first hybrid in 1835. This was only the beginning, and breeders' yearnings for much larger flowers could be realized only when three further species were introduced in later years. *C. florida* and *C. lanuginosa* from China, and *C. patens* from Japan were naturally large-flowered species which allowed the required inflow of suitable genes. From then onwards, hybrids with huge blooms proliferated and such was the hectic pace of breeding that many crosses went unrecorded. The lineage of many favourite clematis is complicated and unknown, not that this concerns many plant lovers who now have a host of flowering gems from which to choose. The passion for new varieties abated around the turn of the twentieth century but the situation was revitalized in the 1950s when professional growers from all over the world took up the challenge again. And so the search goes on, perhaps for plants which are resistant to wilt, or for a large-flowered yellow variety.

Propagation

For the average garden, about half a dozen clematis would seem to be the maximum which can easily be accommodated, but it is surprising how many more can be grown when vertical surfaces are considered. Normally, different varieties are desired but where a particular favourite exists, the lure

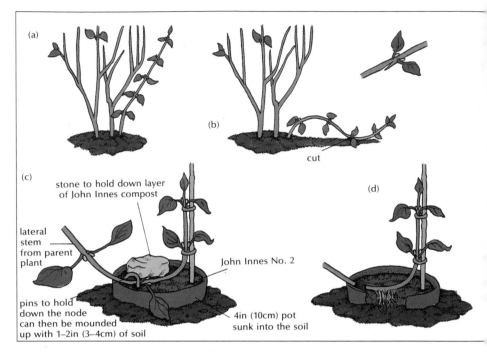

Layering. (a) Choose a suitable stem that will easily bend down to soil level. (b) Make an angled cut 1in (2.5cm) into the node. (c) Peg the layer down firmly into compost and tie the shoot to a bamboo cane. (d) Eventually, sever the rooted layer from the parent plant.

of propagation rears its interesting head. Of course, producing new from the old is done, not only for rearing additional plants, but also as an end in itself and a true cultivator will take up the challenge for the satisfaction which it brings.

Layering is unquestionably the easiest and most reliable method because the parent plant sustains the potential offspring until roots have been formed. When a suitable stem has been identified, a trowelful of soil is removed so that the chosen shoot can be led into a hole and then covered with soil. A peg can be used to secure the stem, or a small rock, but whichever system is employed the aim is to keep the stem in permanent contact with the soil and reasonably moist. Remember that the stem is not

cut from the parent and, ideally, the poin of entry into the ground should be abou 12in (30cm) from its tip and in a positio which is at least partly shaded. Alterna tively, the stem can be pegged into a plar pot (full of soil) which is conveniently place for access. In either case, an adequat rooting system will have formed in about year when it will be time to sever the nev plant from the parent.

The main consideration for this operatio is the choice of a suitable stem which mu be fairly mature and woody because fresl green shoots are too fragile. Early winter the best time to begin layering; suitabl stems are plentiful and a new specimen wi be ready for transplanting in the followir autumn.

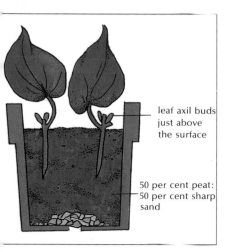

leaf axil buds
just above
the surface

50 per cent peat:
50 per cent sharp
sand

*...ernodal cuttings, which have been
...pped in rooting hormone, are pushed
...mly into the compost. The pot is then
...pt closed until rooting takes place.*

Cuttings, too, are a good means of propagation but it is almost inevitable that some will fail, especially if there are no facilities available. Soft, green shoots can be cut in May or June and inserted into a pot containing sandy compost which, after watering, should be placed in a shaded propagator. Such a facility is extremely useful and enables the cuttings to retain moisture whilst roots are forming. Without using some kind of enclosure, it will be necessary to take hardwood cuttings which can be inserted into the garden soil in the autumn.

Two other points deserve mention to improve the chances of successful rooting. Firstly, the cuttings should be internodal, in other words, the stem should be cut about half-way between leaf joints and not, as is more usual, immediately below a node. The cutting is then inserted to the full length of the stem with the leaf joint just above the

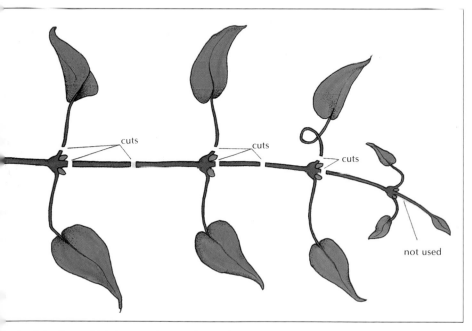

cuts

cuts

cuts

not used

...ogth of vine from which three cuttings can be made.

and experience, there will always be unaccountable failures. The answer is to take more than are needed and if at first you don't succeed. . .

Seed is, of course, the natural means of propagation but unless it is a species which interests you, this can be a very variable business. Even plants grown from the seed of the species and their natural varieties will vary considerably — from almost identical to the parent, to a completely ungarden-worthy plant. Seed harvested from the large flowered hybrids is highly unlikely to produce plants with flowers which are at a

The rich, ruby colouring of 'Niobe' contrasts beautifully with the light yellow stamens.

'Hagley Hybrid' The large, light-pink flowers look better away from full exposure to strong sunshine and the plants are amongst the smallest of the hybrids. Lightly pruned specimens will begin flowering in June with quite large blooms whilst the later ones are smaller but often continue into October.

level of the compost. Secondly, it is vital to reduce the amount of leaf area on the cutting to minimize water loss. Only one leaf is necessary and if this is large, about half of it should be cut off. With all cuttings, it is desirable to dip the cut end of the stem into a hormone rooting powder which protects against fungal problems and also stimulates the formation of roots. The last word on this subject is to emphasize that, for the home gardener, cuttings can never be a precise science and even with equipment

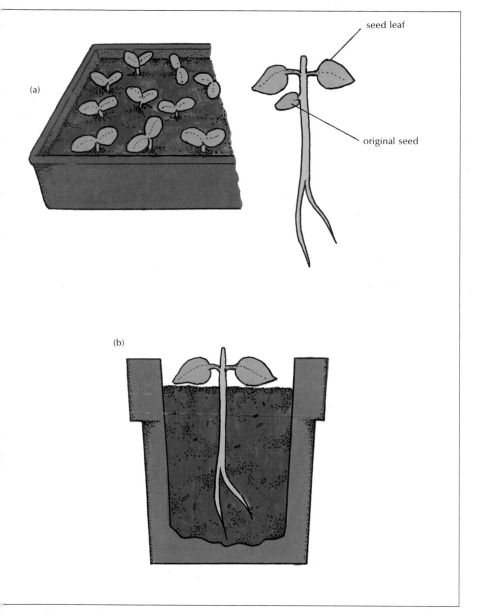

(a)

seed leaf

original seed

(b)

...ting seedlings. (a) When the seedlings are ready to be pricked out, they must be handled by leaves only. (b) Plant the seedlings with the seed leaves only just above the surface of the ...post. After watering, the pot should be kept closed for a few days with a propagator top or ...thene bag. Ventilation is gradually increased, and then the top is finally removed.

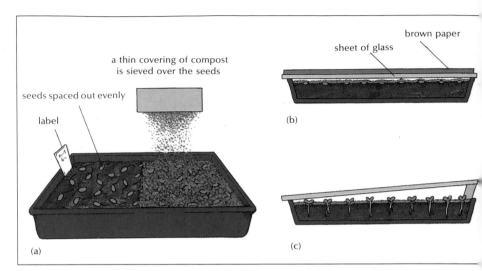

Sowing seed. (a) Fill the tray with compost that is lightly firmed and then soaked before sowing. (b) After watering with a fine rose, cover the seed tray with a sheet of glass, then a sheet of brown paper. For seeds that will take longer to germinate, a piece of slate or tile is more appropriate. Do not allow the surface compost to dry out. (c) Remove the brown paper as soon as the seeds germinate. Increase the ventilation by propping up the glass, and shade from bright sunlight.

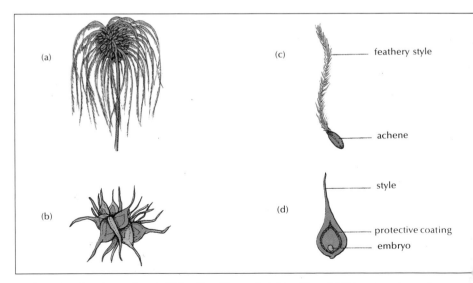

(a) Clematis orientalis seedhead. (b) Seedhead from a hybrid cultivar. (c) This achene has only a thin protective coating and will germinate quickly. (d) This achene has a thicker coating, and will therefore take longer to germinate.

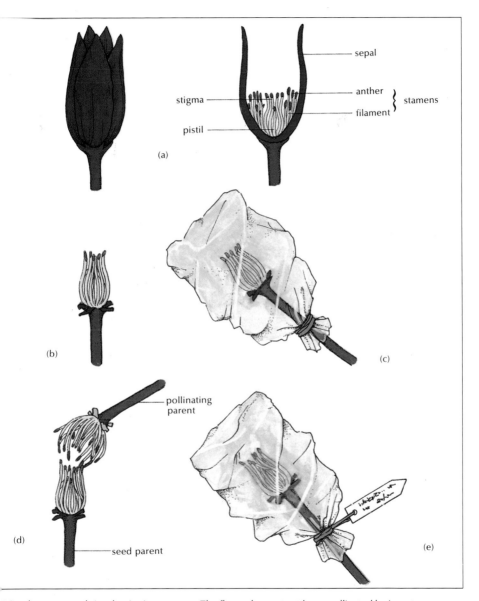

(a)

(b)

(c)

(d)

(e)

sepal

stigma

anther ⎫
        ⎬ stamens
filament ⎭

pistil

pollinating parent

seed parent

) Seed parent sepals just beginning to open. The flower has not yet been pollinated by insects.
) The sepals and stamens have been removed, leaving only the stigma. (c) The stigma
closed in a polythene bag to prevent it being pollinated. (d) Pollen is either brushed on to the
gma with an artist's paintbrush, or transferred directly from the anthers of the pollinating
arent. (e) Replace the polythene bag and leave for a week or two, then remove and leave the
edhead on the plant to ripen. Label clearly, naming the seed parent first.

Comtesse de Bouchaud.

similar to the parent and more probably will not even bear a resemblance. The unreliability of raising new plants from seed is a deterrent to many, but for others the unpredictability is the chief fascination. However, unless you have considerable space, it will be difficult to raise more than a few seedlings and the end result is in the lap of the gods.

The next step is to engage in hybridization and by using deliberate cross-pollination, there can be a breeding programme which culminates in a creditable new variety. It requires enthusiasm, dedication and good fortune, but it is encouraging to note that 'Frances Rivis', 'Niobe' and 'Doctor Ruppel' are all superb cultivars that were raised by amateur growers.

The process simply involves the transfer of pollen from one variety to the seed producing organ of another, but there is no guarantee that quality parents will produce outstanding offspring. The seeds will ripen on the plant in a good year, but otherwise the process can be continued in a cool, dry place indoors. Sowing can take place in the following spring, but the resultant plant must be grown on for another year, at least until such time as their flowers can be judged.

y far the greatest dilemma which faces the rospective clematis grower is choosing om the large number of varieties and pecies in cultivation. The most popular, by ir, are the large-flowered hybrids which re the result of extensive breeding efforts, nost of which have taken place over the ist 150 years. The picture is enhanced, but irther complicated, by the introduction of ew varieties each year from countries all ver the world, including Argentina, anada, Japan, Poland, Russia, Sweden, ne USA and the UK.

There are many characteristics which can e used as a basis for selection — colour, ower shape, ultimate height and vigour, uitability for containers, season of bloom r even rarity value — but these are the rovince of the purchaser. The list which llows gives brief details of some clematis ut it is by no means comprehensive and arieties have been chosen which are eadily available and have a garden per- ormance which is well proven. I must mphasize that any judgement must involve personal viewing because although brief escriptions can be helpful, seeing the lants in flower is the only sound way of hoosing something which will live with ou for many years.

Even a fundamental factor like colour is pen to wide interpretation, as one person's iolet is another's purple. Photographs can e an excellent guide but they too are allible and slight differences in shade can e misleading and cause disappointment. nyone contemplating the purchase of a ong-term garden resident like clematis nould take the trouble to visit specialist urseries or those public gardens which ave notable collections. In this way, the ill splendour can be seen and there is an pportunity to check preferences of aspect nd to ascertain the mature proportions. nother point about the hybrids is that nany are greatly similar and only a keen ye will detect differences.

'Henryi' This used to have the distinctive name of 'Bangholme Belle' and is a lovely creamy white with very large flowers. It is probably the oldest of the large-flowered hybrids, making its appearance in 1858.

The large-flowered plants speak eloquently for themselves, but I do feel prompted to offer recommendations for the small-flowered species and their varieties. There are over 300 species widely dispersed throughout the world but comparatively few are considered to have good garden qualities. The star-shaped flowers of the *montana* are commonly seen smothering the plants in May and June; the *viticella* have nodding blooms reminiscent of *campanula*, and the *alpina*, though more rare, are equally charming. The flowers of C. *armandii*, C. *flammula* and others are pleasantly scented and the species show

nsiderable diversity of flower form and
liage. The small flower size is more than
mpensated for by the sheer number and
e consequent mass of colour.

lematis Varieties

e letters printed after the flower names in
e following lists correspond to those used
Chapter 3 to identify appropriate pruning
ategies.

rge-Flowered Hybrids

ckmanii Superba' (H) A deeper purple
an its stablemate, 'Jackmanii' and equally
olific but perhaps a slightly better quality
wer with broader sepals. In some situa-
ns and in some seasons, there may be a
sceptibility to mildew.

ille de Lyon' (H) Carmine-red flowers
ith slightly darker edges begin to show in
ne and will often continue beyond Sep-
mber. A southern aspect is needed to
courage the late flowers.

he President' (P) This is a slow-growing
ant with a long flowering period and
hough not abundant, the flowers are
ite large. The colour is a royal purple
hich shows well in full sun or partial
ade.

1arie Boisselot' (P) This cultivar also
es under the name of 'Madame Le Coul-
' and is certainly one of the best whites.
e first flowers are huge and although
ose which follow are smaller, they are in
eat profusion. The plants are also exceed-
gly vigorous.

octor Ruppel' (P) A relatively new cle-
atis, introduced in 1975, which has May
d June flowers, strongly coloured in rose-
nk with a carmine bar. The late summer

*e semi-herbaceous C. integrifolia
sociates well with the darker hues of
viticella 'Royal Velours'.*

*'Gypsy Queen' produces a mass of purple
blooms which fade with age.*

blooms vary in colour and are often quite
different from the early ones.

'Elsa Späth' (P) Otherwise called 'Xerxes',
this has good-quality deep-blue flowers that
are displayed over most of the summer on a
modestly sized plant.

'Gypsy Queen' (H) A late-flowering clematis producing masses of purple blooms
which fade somewhat with age but with
dark-red stamens.

'Bee's Jubilee' (P) A superb striped flower
in the 'Nelly Moser' mould with stronger

'Bee's Jubilee' with C. tangutica *flowers and seedheads as companions.*

colours, but the stamens are less striking. It also performs well in a sunny position without much loss of colour.

'Duchess of Edinburgh' (P) Popular for over 100 years and with some unusual features – the double, white blooms are slightly scented and set in a collar of greenish white sepals. The later flowers are usually semi-double and less showy.

'Duchess of Sutherland' (P) A carmine red with a barely discernible lighter bar and a dense cluster of light-cream stamens. June flowers are often semi-double but the main display of single flowers comes in August and September.

'Moonlight' (P) There are no true yellow amongst the large-flowered hybrids but th one is perhaps the nearest – a pale, cream primrose. The plant is far from vigorous ar must be situated in at least partial shade otherwise the subtle colouring will be lost.

'Wada's Primrose' (P) This is a simil colour to the previous clematis and bo varieties flower in late May and June with late flush in September.

I should emphasize that specialist nurseri may have as many as seventy or eigh varieties and as there is often only a sm colour difference with some, it really

dvisable to see them flowering before
making a final decision. You will find that
different catalogues have differing colour
descriptions and it is a case of seeing to
believe.

pecies and their Small-Flowered Varieties

, *alpina* **'Candy' (O)** Unlike the blue-
owered parent species, 'Candy' is a lovely
vo-tone pink with outer sepals which tend
» flatten whilst the innermost are bell-
maped. Like all the *alpina* cultivars, this
ne is extremely hardy and not especially
gorous.

, *alpina* **'Frances Rivis' (O)** This has the
rgest blooms in the *alpina* group, lantern-
maped, blue and pendulous. Again, growth
such that it will never get out of hand.

, *armandii* **(O)** One of the few evergreen
ematis with glossy foliage and the spring
usters of white flowers have a noticeable
anilla fragrance. It should be grown
gainst a sheltered wall to minimize
eather damage but even if it is cut down
y frost, it will normally grow again from
e base.

, *cirrhosa* **(O)** Evergreen and originating
southern Europe, its natural flowering
ne is between November and February
ut this depends on the severity of the
inter. Severe cold will kill the white flow-
s and also the attractive foliage, and in
orthern climates it must have the protec-
on of a warm wall. The variety *C. cirrhosa
alearica*' has fern-like leaves and creamy
hite flowers which are spotted red and
urple on the inside.

florida **'Alba Plena' (H)** A choice plant
ith exquisite greeny, white double blooms
hich are distinctive and long-lasting. The
ant does need a sheltered position and is
amaged by harsh weather.

, *florida* **'Sieboldii' (H)** Outstanding
owers comprising sepals which are off-
hite with a large central cluster of purple,

C. cirrhosa *offers the possibility of winter
colour but needs a warm wall if it is to
flower well.*

petal-like anthers. This variety is quite tender and cold climates will dictate the use of
a greenhouse or conservatory; however,
both this and the previous *florida* are excellent plants for containers.

...he graceful flower heads of C. tangutica *'Lambton Park' are quite unlike those of large-flowered ...brids.*

. macropetala (O) This very robust spe-
...es has really graceful flowers shaped like a
...ghtly open bell. The flowers are a light-blue
fused with purple and the later seedheads
...ok delightful. There are a few *macropetala*
...rieties with white, pink or blue flowers.

. montana (O) This species bears masses
...clustered flowers which are white and
...ghtly scented, and plants will easily grow
...ore than 20ft (6m) high. *C. montana rubens*
...more widely grown and its lighter pink

montana grandiflora *gives a good splash ...*
colour.

varieties – 'Elizabeth', 'Picton's Variety' and
'Tetrarose' – are also scented.

C. tangutica (H) Yellow is the most elusive
clematis colour and it is absent from the
large-flowered hybrids but there are some
species in various shades, of which *tangutica*
is perhaps the most popular. The strength of
colouring is somewhat variable but in the
best examples, the nodding blooms are a rich
yellow and the seedheads are superbly
decorative. The variety 'Lambton Park' is a
good example.

C. texensis (H) As the only true red in the
genus, this species is highly prized and some
notable varieties are widely available –

Duchess of Albany', 'Gravetye Beauty' and
Etoile Rose'. The flowers are most appeal-
ing but the plants do not have the ability to
cling and must be grown through trees or
tied to supports at intervals.

Compared to the large-flowered clematis
hybrids, the species and their cultivars have
small blooms, but their diversity is intri-
guing and they are capable of providing
mass displays in the various seasons. Many
are fragrant, others have pretty seedheads
and, with a few exceptions, they are robust
and without cultivation difficulties.

Varieties for Special Purposes

Containers

Most early summer flowering varieties are
suitable for containers, but especially 'Alice
Fisk' (P), 'Haku Ookan' (P), and 'H.F.
Young' (P). The following mid- and late-
summer varieties are also suitable: 'Elsa
Späth' (P), 'Comtesse de Bouchaud' (H),
'Hagley Hybrid' (H), 'Niobe' (H), 'The President' (P), and the *florida* species (H). For
spring flowers use all the *alpina* and *macropetala* (all H).

North-Facing Walls

In exposed areas use *C. montana* and its
varieties, *rubens*, 'Elizabeth' and 'Picton's
Variety' (all O). In more sheltered conditions
use 'Comtesse de Bouchaud' (H), 'Alice
Fisk' (P), 'Barbara Jackman' (P), 'Bee's Jubi-
lee' (P), 'Doctor Ruppel' (P), 'Duchess of
Edinburgh' (P), 'Henryi' (P), 'Hagley Hybrid'
(H), 'Jackmanii' (H), and 'Jackmanii Superba'
(H), 'Nelly Moser' (P), 'The President' (P),
'Moonlight' (P) and 'Wada's Primrose' (P).

*macropetala with its distinctive, bell-
shaped flowers.*

*'Hagley Hybrid' bears blooms
continuously from June to September.*

You could also use any of the *alpina*,
montana and *macropetala* (all O).

Ground Cover

Many species are suitable for ground cover,
including *alpina*, *macropetala*, *montana*
and *tangutica*.

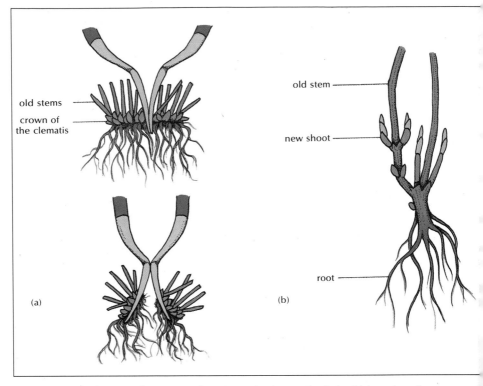

old stem

old stems

crown of
the clematis

new shoot

root

(a)

(b)

(a) Division of herbaceous clematis in early spring, using two garden forks. (b) A section of divided plant ready for replanting.

This book is solely concerned with those clematis which can be classed as climbers but the genus does include a few species which can be described as herbaceous or shrubby. Perhaps the most useful are *C. integrifolia* and its cultivars, having tubular flowers, some of which are fragrant, and growing about 3ft (1m) tall. They will need staking or some means of support and this is also true of *C. recta*, *C. heracleifolia* and *C. jouiniana* which grow much taller although the latter can be allowed to grow horizontally.

These species have flowers that are dissimilar to those of the climbing clematis, and some have large leaves which dwarf the blooms. There are quite a few named varieties of *C. integrifolia*, *Hendersoni* *Olgae* and *Rosea* which will be found i many nurseries. Varieties of *C. heracleifoli* are also widespread, such as, 'Cote d'Azur 'Davidiana', 'Wyevale' and 'Stars', whic all have blue flowers, but 'Mrs Robert Bry don' has off-white blooms.

It could be said that the herbaceou clematis are not to everyone's taste, b they can make an unusual feature in le: formal parts of the garden. All are troubl free and, like other herbaceous plants, th top growth dies to the ground in winte They are also very simply propagated, an suitably large clumps can be divided at th first signs of growth in the spring.